The Academic Achievement of Young Americans

by
J. Stanley Ahmann

Library of Congress Catalog Card Number 83-61783
ISBN 0-87367-196-1
Copyright © 1983 by the Phi Delta Kappa Educational Foundation
Bloomington, Indiana

This fastback is sponsored by the Indiana University Chapter of Phi Delta Kappa, which made a generous contribution toward publication costs.

The chapter sponsors this fastback in recognition of the 75th anniversary of the founding of the School of Education at Indiana University.

Table of Contents

Measuring the Outcomes of Education

Have you ever met a so-called "Renaissance Man"? Some say such a person is broadly educated in arts and letters, and perhaps in the sciences as well. People in this category are rare, but equally rare are individuals of high specific accomplishments such as a world-class gymnast or an internationally renowned stage actor.

In each of the foregoing areas of accomplishment we admire the achievements displayed, for each person has unique and impressive knowledge, understanding, and skill. But are these attributes representative of the entire individual? Probably not. Our "Renaissance Man," in spite of wide-ranging interests coupled with a sweeping command of facts, may be a physical wreck. In contrast, a gymnast with superior body coordination and strength may have poorly developed intellectual skills. Finally, the skilled actor — so effective on stage and so adept at reading the moods of audiences — may have only limited interest in and knowledge of science and technology.

All of the foregoing individuals and their attainments collectively represent major educational outcomes of concern to us. These outcomes are normally classified in three groups: 1) knowledges and understandings (the cognitive group); 2) values, interests, and attitudes (the affective group); and 3) physical movements and abilities (the psychomotor group). As the infant becomes a child and then an adult, all three groups play significant roles. Marked behavioral changes occur, many of which can be traced to planned learning experiences that take place within the framework of our schools. Other experiences are not within the school's purview, and this is as it should be. The components of our total educational enterprise are many and, even though poorly orchestrated at times, they constitute a formidable array of forces from the home and community, with schools as the centerpiece.

Of primary concern to schools are educational outcomes categorized as knowledge, intellectual abilities, and skills. Degrees of student achievement in these areas can be determined by evaluating a wide variety of evidence, including student work products (for example, written assignments), processes demonstrated by students (for example, public speaking), and achievement test scores. The last category includes scores from the traditional essay and objective tests as well as performance tests. Given the importance of verbal and mathematical learning in schools, it is clear that achievement tests play a significant role when measuring the degree to which students are attaining cognitive educational objectives. Indeed, it is not an oversimplification to say that the basic mission of schools is to improve cognitive competence, and that test results are good indicators — but certainly not the only indicators — of how well the educational enterprise is succeeding.

Are Test Scores Declining?

Is it true, as one so often reads, that the test scores of students in our schools are declining at a rapid rate? Many believe that this is the case; if so, it would seem that instead of succeeding, our schools are largely failing in their mission.

Oddly enough, the test data most frequently mentioned to support this conclusion are not from traditional achievement tests but from scholastic aptitude tests administered to college-bound students as a part of the college admission process. For example, the average verbal and mathematical scores on the SAT administered by the College Entrance Examination Board have been reported annually for many years, and the last 15 years have shown a slight decline from year to year. Also, scores from the American College Testing Program (ACT) — the second most widely used college admission tests — are reported annually in the areas of English, mathematics, natural sciences, and social sciences. With the exception of the natural science scores, these tests also show a decline in average achievement.

Informative as these data are, they fail to provide a clear picture of the changes in student performance that are taking place. In the first place, the tests used are designed to predict future academic achievement in college; they are not intended to measure student achievement in a broad array of knowledges and understandings. The content included in the tests is hardly a cross section of the typical school curriculum. Furthermore, the students tested are not a representative sample of all American students. They are a self-selected sample of eleventh- and twelfth-graders and are therefore not typical of the total student population.

If we are to monitor the changes in the levels of achievement of our students, it is clearly necessary to assess these levels (especially cognitive achievement levels) systematically in common, basic learning areas for representative samples of students in the elementary and secondary schools. This has been the role of the National Assessment of Educational Progress (NAEP).

Measuring National Levels of Achievement

The systematic measuring and reporting of what young Americans know and can do is indeed an awesome task. The National Assessment of Educational Progress has had this responsibility since the mid-1960s, thereby providing a useful "national report card" for us to study. During its first 13 years of testing, 25 assessments of achievement in 10 learning areas were conducted; samples totaling over one million individuals were tested; and literally millions of pieces of data were gathered, analyzed, and reported. Because of this we know a good deal about the achievement levels of school-age Americans in common learning areas such as the basic skills, science, and social studies. Innumerable questions remain, however, and the task given NAEP is far from complete.

Table 1 shows a list of the 10 learning areas for which assessments have been developed. Three are basic skills areas (reading, writing, and mathematics), four can be considered general subject-matter areas (science, social studies, citizenship, and career and occupational development), and three can be classified as part of the humanities and fine arts (literature, music, and art). Since 1969-70, six of the learning areas have been assessed three times, three have been assessed twice, and one has been assessed once.

Table 1. Completed Assessments for 10 Learning Areas

Learning Area	Assessments		
	First	Second	Third
Basic Skill Areas			
Reading	1970-71	1974-75	1979-80
Writing	1969-70	1973-74	1978-79
Mathematics	1972-73	1977-78	1981-82
General Subject-Matter Areas			
Science	1969-70	1972-73	1976-77
Social Studies	1971-72	1975-76	1981-82
Citizenship	1969-70	1975-76	1981-82
Career and Occupational Development	1973-74		
Humanities and Fine Arts Areas			
Literature	1970-71	1979-80	
Art	1974-75	1978-79	
Music	1971-72	1978-79	

Note: A fourth assessment of reading and writing achievement is scheduled for 1983-84, and a fourth assessment of mathematics and science achievement is scheduled for 1985-86.

Each assessment is the product of many years of work by a large number of educators, specialists, and concerned laymen from all over the country. As members of committees, these people identify the educational objectives for each learning area that they feel young Americans should be achieving as a part of their formal education. These are consensus objectives and therefore do not include all aspects of each learning area. On the other hand, they do represent the main body of the learning area and the central ideas about which schools should be concerned.

For most objectives, test exercises suitable for 9-, 13-, and 17-year-olds (and sometimes young adults) are carefully developed. Because each exercise is designed to be a direct reflection of a designated objective, the degree to which young Americans successfully respond to an exercise provides information about how well the objective is being achieved. The study of wrong answers offers valuable insights into the origin of faulty learning and suggests possible remedial actions.

Many of the exercises have a cognitive emphasis and resemble the common paper-and-pencil test items used in the classrooms today.

Other exercises require the student to do more than simply select a correct answer. For example, the student may be required to give reasons for an answer, to manipulate apparatus, to draw a picture, to sing a song, or to write an essay. These exercises are often individually administered and are scored according to carefully drawn criteria.

After the exercises have passed an intensive review to guarantee that they adequately reflect the objectives of concern, they are administered to probability samples of students in each age group. The individuals included in these samples are chosen in such a way that the results of their assessment can be generalized to an entire national population. No one is tested more than once, but some exercises are used a second or third time when a learning area is reassessed.

The second and third assessments are of crucial importance. About one-half of the exercises from the previous assessment are thoroughly reexamined in terms of pertinent objectives, and they are then administered unchanged to a new sample of young Americans from the proper age group. The second and third assessments reveal changes in levels of achievement, providing significant information about achievement trends that may exist. A learning area is usually assessed every four or five years, with the basic skills being tested more frequently.

For each exercise in each learning area, NAEP determines the percentage of students in a given age group who have answered the question accurately or performed the task required successfully. In addition, percentages of success are also reported for groups of related exercises, such as those associated with a common educational objective or based on the same kind of subject matter. Finally, percentages of success are reported for easily identified subgroups of students in each age group. Specifically, scores are reported by geographic region of the country, size and type of community in which students live, level of parental education, gender, and ethnic classification of the students. Use of these classifications provides rough but striking profiles of student achievement.

Achievement Profiles for Various Student Groups

By 1975 all 10 learning areas had been assessed at least once. The mountains of data resulting from these assessments constituted a group

11

of bench marks to be used for comparison with the results of later assessments to measure the changes in levels of achievement that occurred in the last half of the 1970s and the first years of the 1980s. Here is what the bench mark data told us.

Regions of the Country. A fairly large degree of consistency existed from one learning area to another in the differences in levels of achievement found among students from various parts of the country. For example, in all learning areas reported, the levels of performance in the Northeast region were usually slightly higher than those of the other three regions. The levels of performance in the Central region were also above the national average, whereas the achievement levels for the West varied depending on the age group considered. In contrast, the achievement levels in the Southeast usually fell below the national level. In all instances the differences among the regions were comparatively small.

Size and Type of Community. Students living in communities of various sizes and types differed noticeably from each other in levels of achievement in all learning areas. Those living in the affluent suburbs were, as expected, superior in achievement; those from the inner city trailed all other groups by a large margin. Rural youth did somewhat better than inner-city youth, but still performed below the national average.

Gender. Male-female differences in achievement varied, depending on the learning area. For example, female students generally achieved at higher levels in learning areas with a heavy verbal component, such as reading, writing, and literature. Male students achieved at a consistently higher level in science. In the case of mathematics, no pattern seems to exist, except that female students had a better command of the computational aspect of arithmetic at age 13, but failed to achieve as well as men when they became young adults. Also, the music achievement of female students exceeded somewhat that of males, but the drawing scores in the art assessment were quite similar for both groups.

Educational Level of Parent. Because the educational level of the parents of the student is a respectable measure of socioeconomic status, it was not surprising to find sharp differences among students whose parents had widely different levels of education. In all learning areas, student achievement increased markedly and with striking consistency

12

as the level of parental education rose. This trend was especially strong in the basic skill learning areas.

Ethnic Groups. Wide differences in levels of achievement existed among students in the major ethnic groups. The achievement levels of black students fell well below the national average, while those for white students were above it. The evidence available for Hispanic students showed that they also fell below the national average when achievement levels in five learning areas (reading, mathematics, science, social studies, and career and occupational development) were considered; this deficit, however, was generally not as pronounced as that found for blacks.

A Synopsis. In many ways the profiles reported in the foregoing paragraphs are not surprising. The differences that existed among the various subgroups were often found to be in the direction expected. On the other hand, many times the *sizes* of the differences were unusually large. The patterns that emerged clearly revealed that some schools faced very different teaching-learning situations than others. The mix of students in a given school is determined by forces largely outside the control of the educational enterprise, and it may create either a highly supportive instructional situation or a most perplexing one for the teachers involved.

Descriptions of Student Achievement: The Bench Mark Data

As instructive as it is to examine the achievement profiles for various student subgroups in order to discover which achieved relatively well and which did not, this information does not describe to any useful degree exactly what most students know and can do. What is needed are descriptive statements delineating the knowledges and skills in each learning area that are possessed by most students in each age group. This list, along with a list of knowledges and skills that few students possess, would reveal to us, in practical terms, the accomplishments of our educational system. Because the test exercises used by NAEP were direct outgrowths of commonly used educational objectives, it was possible to prepare such lists by examining the bench mark test data to ascertain whether many or few students achieved each objective.

The statements describing what 9-year-olds, 13-year-olds, and

13

17-year-olds in the nation knew and could do in the 10 learning areas assessed have been greeted more often with cries of distress than with expressions of pleasure. If one wished to find evidence that Jane or Johnny were less than perfect learners, it was certainly possible to do so. On the other hand, there was ample evidence that students were learning significant amounts of subject matter and that, as young adults, they were able to retain a great part of it. The following highlights for each age group provides a brief overview of what the bench mark data indicated these students were learning in the early 1970s.

Nine-year-olds: Mostly Fourth-Graders. During their first few years of schooling, 9-year-olds focused on the basics, such as reading and writing skills. They could read simple stories and write letters to their friends, and they knew a variety of subject-matter facts. Moreover, they were tolerant of other people's cultural differences and believed in an orderly society.

Many 9-year-olds (more than two-thirds) could:

- Tell time
- Add two-digit numbers
- Comprehend the properties of zero
- Read and comprehend literal facts in simple, brief stories
- Read short descriptions of people or things and infer how the person was feeling or what object was being described
- Write without making punctuation or word choice errors
- Identify the names and descriptions of some common jobs
- Describe in a general way how the president of the United States is selected
- Improvise rhythms and follow rhythmic patterns while singing
- Draw in perspective by showing figures progressively higher on the picture plane

On the other hand, fewer 9-year-olds (less than one-third) could:

- Subtract three- and four-digit numbers
- Multiply and divide numbers, or understand fractions
- Determine the main idea in a reading passage
- Express a thoughtful reaction to a piece of literature
- Understand detailed written instructions or directions

- Organize and elaborate on ideas in writing
- Write essays free of misspelled words, sentence fragments, and run-on sentences
- Identify what an atom is
- Describe the basic functions of the executive and legislative branches of government
- Read musical notation

Thirteen-year-olds: Mostly Eighth-Graders. Thirteen-year-olds could read, write, add, subtract, divide, and multiply when told to do so. They did not, however, use these skills by themselves to solve everyday problems. They had the skills and knowledges necessary to accomplish routine tasks at home and at school. They had also developed some study skills and knew a variety of useful facts, but the idea that they could use these skills and knowledges to make their daily lives more interesting and productive was not always obvious to them.

Many 13-year-olds (more than two-thirds) could:

- Add, subtract, multiply, and divide whole numbers and decimals
- Multiply fractions
- Read and comprehend short, straightforward materials
- Read for main ideas and understand some elements of literary language
- Write rudimentary social and business letters
- Write a cluster of two or three related ideas
- Use basic reference materials
- Describe the functions of the major parts of the body
- Identify the basic functions of the court system
- Identify the names and sounds of most musical instruments

In contrast, fewer 13-year-olds (less than one-third) could:

- Understand basic probability and statistics
- Choose the most economical buy in a supermarket
- Infer meaning from sophisticated passages of prose
- Evaluate poetry and prose thoughtfully
- Express feelings in writing

- Understand the transfer of energy
- Describe what to do when a person faints
- Explain the relationships among the branches of the U.S. government
- Identify classical composers
- Show perspective by drawing objects larger and smaller to indicate distance

Seventeen-year-olds: Mostly Eleventh-Graders. Seventeen-year-olds had mastered the basic skills and knew many specific facts in all school subjects but had difficulty organizing and applying what they knew. They had some knowledge of the world of work, had thought about their futures, and knew what attitudes and behaviors were expected of them in our society. They knew a number of facts about our government and legal system, as well as some specific scientific facts. They had difficulty reading long passages and had limited vocabularies when writing. They could read, write, and compute in well-structured situations but had difficulty applying their knowledge in new situations.

Many 17-year-olds (more than two-thirds) could:

- Multiply fractions and reduce them to lowest terms
- Solve simple word problems requiring multiplication
- Evaluate simple algebraic expressions and solve first-degree equations and inequalities
- Read and understand short, straightforward materials such as newspaper advertisements and telephone bills
- Use a map legend and book index
- Demonstrate mastery of the mechanics of writing
- Write a note explaining a problem
- Understand basic facts about nutrition, illness, and disease
- Describe some of the functions and limits of the executive and judicial branches of government
- Identify musical symbols and terms

On the other hand, fewer 17-year-olds (less than one-third) could:

- Calculate the area of a square given its perimeter
- Simplify algebraic expressions

16

- Write high quality essays
- Identify oxygen and silicon as the components that make up most of the earth's mass
- Comprehend quantitative relationships in physics and chemistry
- Describe geographic relationships
- Explain the structure and function of the legislative branch of government
- Describe how farm prices seek their own level in a free market system
- Improvise or repeat a harmonic line of music
- Sing from printed music with acceptable rhythm and pitch

The foregoing is a mere sample of the hundreds of statements that could be made about the degree of scholastic achievement of school-age Americans as of the mid-1970s. In many ways the statements are quite informative — certainly more informative than scores representing the number of correct responses to a large group of test items.

When evaluating general descriptions of the achievements of students in a specified age group, we should remind ourselves again that some groups of students surpassed others in all 10 learning areas. Widespread differences commonly existed among the subgroups within each age group. For instance, those groups whose levels of academic achievement were relatively low when compared to national averages usually included students who lived in rural or inner-city neighborhoods, who were black, who lived in the Southeastern part of the country, or who had parents with little formal schooling. Conversely, students in those groups whose levels of achievement were relatively high lived in affluent suburbs of metropolitan areas, lived in the Northeast or Central part of the country, and had parents with better educational backgrounds.

Beyond the Bench Marks

Such are the achievement bench marks that existed during the first half of the 1970s. What has happened since that time? Have any pronounced changes taken place? Are the student groups who achieved poorly still trailing their peers, or are some improving relative to national levels of achievement? Are the high-achieving students still doing well, or are they slipping? Most important of all, are the overall trends in achievement moving upward or downward, and are these trends different for the various learning areas?

Complete answers to these questions are not available, but the second and third assessments conducted by NAEP provide data that show a dynamic situation. There are notable gains and losses, some of which are distinct surprises.

Changes in Levels of Achievement: A Mixture of Gains and Losses

We live in remarkable times indeed. Consider for a moment the seeming contradictions we face daily as consumers. We find, for example, that automobiles are becoming smaller, but their prices are steadily increasing. At the same time, personal computers are more powerful and efficient than ever, and yet their prices are declining. Even food prices are puzzling in that they rarely drop and often rise in spite of huge surpluses of farm commodities in storage.

While contradictions such as these abound in our daily lives, are we also likely to find them when we measure the achievement of our students? Do significant gains and losses always follow when teaching efforts and educational dollars are redirected? In recent years, for example, much concern has been focused on student command of the basic skills, particularly reading and mathematics at the elementary school level. For this and other reasons, costly federal assistance programs have been installed and minimum competency testing programs administered. Now it is appropriate to ask whether achievement in such learning areas as reading, writing, and mathematics is improving.

In contrast, the emphasis on science instruction in the schools was generally less in the 1970s than in earlier years. Shortages of qualified science and mathematics teachers were widely reported, budgets for science supplies and materials dwindled, and high school graduation requirements for science eased. In view of this, should we expect the levels of science achievement to have fallen?

In an effort to answer these questions, beginning in the 1970s and continuing in the 1980s, NAEP repeatedly measured levels of achievement of school-age Americans in reading, writing, mathematics, science, social studies, citizenship, music, and art. These data revealed distinct upward and downward trends, some of which were more than a little unexpected.

Basic Skills: Reading, Writing, and Mathematics

Levels of Achievement in Reading. NAEP measured levels of achievement in reading three times, in 1970-71, 1974-75, and 1979-80. The same reading exercises were administered in all three assessments so that changes in levels of performance could be measured over the nine-year period for all three age groups.

The exercises measured three different aspects of reading: literal comprehension, inferential comprehension, and reference skills. Literal comprehension exercises required the students to remember the exact meaning of the material read, whereas inferential comprehension test items required them to infer from a reading passage ideas that were not explicitly stated. Reference skills exercises required students to demonstrate where and how to find information.

The pattern of change is mixed. Nationally, the overall reading performance level for 9-year-olds rose 3.9%, whereas the reading performance for 13-year-olds did not change appreciably in the 1970s. However, the performance of 13-year-olds in literal comprehension improved slightly (1.6%). Of special interest were the 17-year-olds — that group scheduled to graduate from high school in a year or less. The reading achievement picture for these students differed from that of their younger classmates, especially in the case of those exercises requiring inferential comprehension. Here the national level of achievement of 17-year-olds fell about 2%.

Of concern to many educators are the student responses to reading and literature test items that required relatively complex interpretive and analytical skills. For example, in one exercise 17-year-olds were asked to substantiate their claims about the mood of a literary passage by turning back to the text for evidence. In 1971, 51% of the students wrote adequate analyses, but in 1980 only 41% were able to do so for the passage in question. This drop of 10%, as well as other evidence in the reading and literature assessments, showed a decline in the ability of 17-year-olds to handle test items requiring analytical skills. In several test items of this type, only 5% to 10% of the students displayed strong analytic ability.

On the positive side, several subgroups of students made significant gains in certain reading categories over the nine years of the assessment, even though their reading achievement level was below the national average. For example, 9- and 13-year-olds from the Southeast made significant gains in literal comprehension, and 9-year-olds in the Southeast also improved in inferential comprehension and reference skills. Moreover, black 9- and 13-year-olds made unusual gains in literal and inferential comprehension as well as in reference skills. Finally, 9-year-olds attending schools in rural communities made important gains in literal and inferential comprehension and in reference skills. The largest gain of all was made by 9-year-old black students, whose overall reading performance improved 9.9% in nine years; 13-year-old black students gained 4.2%.

Though still reading below national levels, Hispanic 9-year-olds improved their reading achievement 5.3% between 1975 and 1980. This improvement was particularly pronounced for those living in large cities, where achievement rose 8.4%. Although the overall reading performance of 13- and 17-year-old Hispanos did not change very much in the last half of the 1970s, 13-year-olds in large cities improved 5.9% in literal comprehension, and the inferential comprehension skills of city-dwelling 17-year-olds improved by 7.1%. In summary, students from an important number of low-achieving groups tended to improve their reading performance during the 1970s and, as a result, narrowed the gap between themselves and the national average.

Levels of Achievement in Writing. In each of its three assessments of writing skills in the 1970s, NAEP required students to prepare writing samples such as essays and letters. These were evaluated for overall quality, rhetorical effectiveness, coherence, cohesion, syntactic fluency, and mechanical correctness. This comprehensive evaluation showed that the three age groups performed differently over the decade and that each group seemed to have its own pattern of strengths and weaknesses. On the other hand, some uniformities were found. For example, 13- and

17-year-olds either improved their expressive writing skills or the skills remained at about the same level during the 1970s, while persuasive and descriptive skills appeared to be declining. Also, an analysis of writing errors did not reveal any major changes over the nine years of the assessments for any age group.

While approximately three-fourths of the 17-year-olds demonstrated at least minimal ability to write complete sentences and paragraphs with few mechanical errors, about 10% to 25% had very serious problems with written English. In general, 17-year-olds were much less successful with persuasive writing exercises that involved logic, analysis, and other complex skills; there is evidence that by 1979 these skills had declined. Furthermore, in writing exercises designed to measure explanatory, expressive, and persuasive writing abilities, there was a large variation (15% to 75%) across the different tasks in the percentage of 17-year-olds judged as competent or better. It must be concluded that many 17-year-olds were unable to write for different purposes and different audiences.

Improvement was noted in the achievement of certain subgroups of low-achieving students. For instance, black 13- and 17-year-olds improved either absolutely or relatively on all required writing tasks. Furthermore, 17-year-olds from economically disadvantaged inner-city areas made steady gains over the nine-year period. Nine- and 13-year-olds from these areas did not fare as well. Few improvements of consequence were found in the achievement of other subgroups that typically fall below the national average.

Levels of Achievement in Mathematics. Levels of achievement in mathematics were measured on a national scale in 1972-73, 1977-78, and again in 1981-82, covering a span of nine years. These assessments included exercises that measured mathematical knowledge, skills, understanding, and applications. Mathematical knowledge exercises emphasized the recall of facts and definitions, while exercises in mathematial skills required the student to use specific algorithms and manipulate mathematical symbols. In contrast, mathematical understanding exercises were based on higher-level cognitive processes in that they required translation between symbols and words. Mathematical application exercises involved the use of mathematical knowledge, skills, and understanding to solve problems; the student had to select the appropriate facts, algorithms, or understandings and apply them correctly.

The overall performance in mathematics of 9-year-olds was relatively stable over the nine years covered by the three assessments, neither declining nor improving significantly. The performance of 13-year-olds declined (2%) between the first two assessments, and then improved (about 4%) between the second and third — a solid gain. The performance pattern of the 17-year-olds differed from those of the other two age groups in that mathematics achievement dropped 4% between the first and second assessment and remained virtually unchanged between the second and third.

The improvement by 13-year-olds during the four years between the second and third assessments was impressive, but much of this gain is reflected in their performance on rather routine mathematical functions, such as those requiring computation and recognition. In general, students of all age levels made only modest gains — or no gains at all — on problems measuring higher-order understanding or applications of mathematics.

It should also be noted that achievement by 13-year-olds improved in every content area in mathematics; these included number and numeration, variables and relations, geometry, measurement, probability and statistics, and graphs and tables. In the case of geometry, for example, performance consistently rose on exercises that could be solved intuitively without much formal knowledge of geometric principles. Those exercises requiring knowledge of specific geometric theorems showed about as many declines as increases, and the increases were relatively modest.

Knowledge of the metric system improved dramatically between the second and third assessments. Thirteen-year-olds led all age groups with a 9% increase, followed by 17-year-olds with a 4% increase and 9-year-olds with an increase of 2%. Incidentally, there was a general decrease in all age groups with respect to knowledge of the English measurement system.

Although the average mathematics performance of black and Hispanic students continued to be below the national average, 13-year-olds in these groups made substantial gains in mathematics (about 7%)

between the second and third assessments. Moreover, these gains were usually substantially larger than those made by their white peers. In general, the most significant gains were made on exercises requiring basic cognitive processes rather than higher-order learning. In addition, 13-year-old students attending inner-city schools registered larger gains than the national sample on exercises dealing with skills, understanding, and application of mathematics.

Looking at the mathematics results across all age groups tested, one finds evidence that our schools were reasonably successful in teaching routine computational and measurement skills and basic knowledge about numbers and geometry. Also there were positive changes in knowledge and skills, not only in numerical computation but also in geometry and measurement. On the other hand, it appears that schools thus far have taught only a small percentage of students how to analyze mathematical problems and how to apply mathematical concepts in solving problems.

Comparing High and Low Achievers in the Basic Skills. Examining NAEP data in the basic skills reveals some interesting comparisons between good and poor students in terms of their respective changes in levels of achievement. This is done by using the results of an early assessment to identify students who achieved well (top one-fourth) in a learning area and those who achieved poorly (bottom one-fourth) in that area, and then comparing the two groups in terms of changes in levels of achievement found in a later assessment. The top and bottom achievement categories cut across socioeconomic lines. In other words, the top one-fourth includes students from disadvantaged as well as advantaged backgrounds, as does the bottom one-fourth.

In the case of reading and mathematics, a comparison of high and low achievers shows that, in general, students in the bottom one-fourth realized *greater* gains in the second half of the 1970s than those in the top one-fourth. Most of the gains were in reading for 9-year-olds (about 5%), but some occurred for 13-year-olds as well.

Black students in the lowest one-fourth who were in the normal grade level for 9-, 13-, and 17-year-olds (that is, fourth, eighth, and eleventh grade, respectively) showed increased achievement in both reading and mathematics. Moreover, black fourth-graders in the top one-fourth raised their reading and mathematics scores, and black eighth-graders in the top one-fourth also improved in reading. Often, achievement gains by black students in the normal grade level for their age exceeded those of white students in the same grades. On the other hand, both white and black 17-year-olds in the eleventh grade who were in the top one-fourth suffered substantial losses in achievement in mathematics.

Content Areas: Science and Social Studies/Citizenship

Levels of Achievement in Science. The three assessments in biological and physical science took place in 1969-70, 1972-73, and 1976-77. A noticeable decline in achievement occurred for each of the three age groups from the first assessment to the second and, in the case of the 17-year-olds, from the second assessment to the third. The levels of achievement for 9- and 13-year-olds at the third assessment were similar to those of the second assessment.

Declines in levels of achievement in physical science were more pronounced than those in biological science, especially for 17-year-olds. In the case of 9- and 13-year-olds, achievement in biological science changed very little across the three assessments.

When comparing achievement levels in biological science with those in physical science, it should be noted that many of the test items in the former simply required recall of information. However, the majority of the items in physical science required that students not only recall needed information but also use it appropriately in terms of the requirements of a stated problem. This difference in difficulty probably accounts in part for the fact that, in the 1976-77 assessment, the average percent correct for all biological science test items for 17-year-olds was 52%, while the average percent correct for all physical science test items for the same group was 44%. Moreover, the decline in level of achievement in physical science for 1969-1977 for this age group was noticeably greater than the decline in level of achievement in test items dealing with biological science for the same time span. Indeed, there is reason to believe that the decline of the higher-level science skills is at least twice that of the lower-level science skills.

The relative achievement of many of the subgroups of students tested

25

did not change appreciably over the seven-year period during which the assessments were conducted. However, students at the three age levels who live in rural communities did improve in science achievement from 1969-70 to 1976-77. Also, black 13-year-olds improved in physical science achievement from the second to the third assessment. In contrast, substantial losses in science achievement were found for high-achieving (top one-fourth) white 9-year-olds in the fourth grade, white 13-year-olds in the eighth grade, and both white and black 17-year-olds in the eleventh grade.

Levels of Achievement in Social Studies/Citizenship. The assessments in social studies in 1971-72 and 1975-76 included knowledges, skills, and attitudes in this learning area. Assessments in citizenship were completed in 1969-70 and 1975-76, measuring achievement components such as student concern for the well-being of others; support for law and the rights of others; participation in civic improvement; knowledge of the structure and function of government; and understanding of world, national, and local government. Obviously the social studies and citizenship learning areas as defined by NAEP are highly related, and the results of these assessments can be easily combined.

In general no change was found for 9-year-olds in social studies achievement, but the achievement of 13-year-olds declined slightly while the achievement of 17-year-olds declined significantly. At the same time, some of the subgroups of students improved their relative position with regard to achievement in this learning area. For example, 9-year-old black students showed improvement in four years while 9-year-old white students did not. Among the 17-year-olds, the achievement of Hispanic students and those living in the West declined less than the entire group. Also, 17-year-olds living in affluent suburbs showed larger drops in achievement in social studies than did the nation as a whole.

Thirteen- and 17-year-olds living in rural communities revealed a tendency to improve their achievement in citizenship when compared to the nation as a whole. On the other hand, practically all of the other subgroups held their relative position during the period covered by the several assessments of social studies and citizenship.

Political knowledge and attitudes were measured in both social studies assessments as well as in the citizenship assessments for such topics as constitutional rights, respect for others, structure and function of government, and the political process. Analysis of NAEP data reveals striking declines in the level of achievement for both 13- and 17-year-olds, especially the latter. A decline of more than 10% was reported for 17-year-olds with respect to their knowledge of the structure and function of government, and a decline of slightly more than 5% occurred for 13-year-olds in this category. In the case of the political process category, the 17-year-olds experienced a decline of more than 6%, while the 13-year-olds had a decline of slightly more than 4%. Declines in achievement were generally smaller on exercises concerned with constitutional rights and respect for others.

Illustrative of students' conceptual level when asked to explain in simple terms the basic concept of democracy was the statement of one student who said: "It's where people get ripped off, I think by Congress." Another more perceptive statement came from a student who described democracy as "a government of discovery." On a more positive note, there was a 20% increase in understanding by 13-year-olds that police may not incarcerate arrested persons idefinitely while they collect evidence against them. On the other hand, there was a decline of more than 16% in the ability of 13-year-olds to provide adequate reasons to either support or reject the right of assembly in all situations. Given the importance of this constitutional right, it is disconcerting to see a decline in students' understanding of this right.

Fine Arts: Music and Art

Levels of Achievement in Music. Exercises used in the first assessment of music achievement in 1971-72 were based on five objectives. Since only three of these objectives were also used in the second assessment in 1978-79, it is possible only to compare changes in levels of music achievement on the following objectives:

1. Value music as an important realm of human experience
2. Identify the elements and expressive controls of music
3. Identify and classify music historically and culturally.

The assessments show that there was a tendency for the music achievement of 9- and 17-year-olds to decline during the seven-year period. Insofar as the 13-year-olds are concerned, little or no change in music achievement occurred in the aggregate. On the other hand, there is evidence that the 13-year-olds valued music as an important realm of human experience to a greater degree at the time of the second assessment in 1978-79 than they did seven years earlier. For 9- and 17-year-olds, achievement slipped most in their ability to identify the elements and expressive controls of music. Finally, knowledge about music history and style did not change significantly over time for any of the three age groups.

Some of the subgroups that traditionally achieved below the national average in each assessment reversed that tendency with regard to their ability to "value music as an important realm of human experience." Achieving *above* the national average in 1978-79 with respect to exercises associated with this objective were 9-, 13-, and 17-year-olds who live in the Southeast, 13-year-olds who were black or who lived in rural areas, and black 17-year-olds. This better-than-average achievement by these subgroups did not occur for the other two objectives used in both assessments.

Levels of Achievement in Art. Assessments of art achievement took place in 1974-75 and in 1978-79. These assessments were based on five major objectives, namely, the ability to:

1. Perceive and respond to aspects of art
2. Value art as an important realm of human experience
3. Produce works of art
4. Know about art
5. Make and justify judgments about the aesthetic merit and quality of works of art.

Once again there were significant declines in achievement between assessments for 13- and 17-year-olds. This decline was particularly pronounced in achievement of the second objective, valuing art. In this area 13-year-olds declined more than 3% and 17-year-olds declined 4%. One interpretation of these declines is that teenagers were less willing to accept all kinds of art, not simply the traditional forms.

Although only a few test items measured knowledge of art, there was reason to believe that students did not possess widespread knowledge in this area. Most often fewer than half the students recognized famous works or knew when, where, or by whom they were created. In addition, the assessment results suggest that knowledge of art decreased among 9- and 13-year-olds.

Although the primary focus of art education at all levels of schooling is to provide art-making experiences, the assessment results show that the majority of students could not draw or design well. When confronted with the task of drawing an angry person, 15% of the 13-year-olds and 19% of the 17-year-olds succeeded in doing so in 1978-79, a slight improvement over their 1974-75 efforts. But the percentages of teenagers who showed commercial design skill by creating an acceptable design for a cereal box dropped by 6% for 13-year-olds and by 2% for 17-year-olds. In 1978-79, 22% of the 13-year-olds and 30% of the 17-year-olds created acceptable designs.

Many subgroups of students held the same relative positions with regard to national average levels for art achievement as they did for academic subjects such as reading, mathematics, and science. Socioeconomic factors evidently have a bearing on achievement in this area, and students whose parents had some education beyond high school or who lived in affluent suburbs were usually above the national levels for art achievement. Students from lower socioeconomic environments tended to fall below the national average in this learning area.

Evolving Trends in Achievement

Even the most casual examination of NAEP data showing changes in levels of achievement during the 1970s leads to a number of conclusions. The overall picture for 9-year-olds, for example, is promising. On the other hand, the outlook for 13-year-olds (with the possible exception of mathematics) is less encouraging, and that for 17-year-olds is quite disturbing. Despite these declines, it is most heartening to observe the repeated gains in achievement in many learning areas for student groups that typically fall below the national average. Prominent among these are black and Hispanic 9-year-olds; their gains in reading represent an exciting success story for our schools. Also, it is reassuring to document the increasing academic achievement of students living in economically disadvantaged areas; even though they still perform below the national average, they are improving noticeably.

There are a number of signs that students who achieve relatively poorly in an early assessment of a learning area (that is, the bottom one-fourth of those tested) are realizing greater gains than those who initially achieved very well (the top one-fourth of those tested). In addition, among both high and low achievers, black students are more likely than white students to show gains, although the overall performance of blacks remains below that of whites.

The reading assessment data contain a number of bright spots, particularly for young students who are economically disadvantaged. Many are less able readers and populate the bottom one-fourth of those tested in early assessments. The last reading assessment shows that both 9- and 13-year-old students in the bottom one-fourth improved their reading achievement quite significantly in five years. It would be gratifying if the picture was as encouraging in the case of achievement in the content areas and the fine arts.

A vexing problem that appears regularly is the uneven achievement in tasks requiring more than recall of information or the near-mechanical use of a skill. In the basic skills, for instance, there is disquieting evidence that students — especially 17-year-olds — have not mastered a wide variety of higher-order skills, such as the ability to apply facts and principles in new situations or to analyze a complex situation and draw conclusions about it. Achievement levels for both inferential comprehension exercises in reading and application exercises in mathematics are too low and are not rising. The dismal picture enlarges when one examines the efforts of 17-year-olds to write persuasive prose involving skills in logic and analysis, or when one studies their responses to physical science exercises that demand the application of scientific principles or the interpretation of data.

Whether it is good news or bad news, these nationwide assessments of achievement in the 1970s do identify fundamental educational trends. Furthermore, these trends are national in scope, with modest differences from one region of the country to another, and they vary according to the learning area under study and the type of student tested.

The variations among different types of students can be dramatic, and changes can occur in as short a period as three or four years.

Thus our "national report card" is a steadily unfolding picture. It is fair to say that it is not as good as we hoped, but not as bad as we feared. What, then, are we going to do about it?

Toward Better Schools

Who is a good reader? If folklore is to be believed, it is certainly not someone named "Johnny." Nevertheless, it is possible to build a profile of good readers. A list of common characteristics has emerged from studies undertaken by NAEP and is worth examining. Some of these are fairly commonplace, others a bit unusual.

Good readers are, for the most part, students who do more homework, who do not spend an excessive amount of time watching television, and who clearly enjoy reading. They customarily read often during their spare time and have a taste for fiction as well as nonfiction. Moreover, superior reading ability is generally found among female students, white students, students who attend schools in the affluent suburbs, and students with parents having formal education beyond the high school level.

Knowing these characteristics, how do we go about "manufacturing" more good readers in the future? It is no easy task, that is certain. After all, the foregoing profile of good readers is a summary of the consistent associations found between levels of reading achievement and a variety of background characteristics of the students tested. Whether there are cause-and-effect relationships between reading achievement and these characteristics is still not proven, even though high degrees of association are continually found. If there were causal relationships, we could produce better readers — ridiculous as this sounds — by moving families to affluent suburbs, junking their television sets, increasing the amount of homework for all students, and enrolling parents in college.

NAEP data can establish the degree to which achievement levels are consistently associated with student characteristics and nothing more. Association does not establish causality. Therefore, we must be very cautious about drawing inferences about particular relationships, no matter how significant they are or how often they are found. Nevertheless, such massive amounts of data do need interpretation.

Panels of educators and concerned lay citizens have examined assessment findings in each learning area very carefully and have attempted to interpret them. These panels addressed three questions:

1. What are the critical findings revealed by the assessments?
2. What are the underlying causes of the achievement patterns found?
3. What can the schools do to improve student achievement in the future?

Answering these questions is extremely difficult, and the interpretations expressed are by no means unanimously supported. Members of the panels are forced to engage in a good deal of speculation — intelligent speculation, it turns out — about all parts of the assessment data, the associations between achievement levels and student characteristics, the operating conditions of today's schools, and the pressures exerted by society as a whole. At best, distilling all of these into a small number of cogent statements useful to school administrators and teachers is a tough job. After all, few — maybe none — of the achievement patterns found by NAEP are characteristic of *all* of our schools. Instead, each school is shaped by the dynamic interactions between the homes from which the students come and the organizations within the community in which they live. All of these forces contribute to the education or miseducation of students to some degree.

In spite of all this, the work of the many NAEP panels has been important and useful. One of the most far-reaching conclusions after analyzing the NAEP data is that student gains in achievement in the 1970s most often occurred when lower-order cognitive skills (for example, recall of information) were involved, but some decline was observed when test items required higher-order skills (for example, problem-solving ability). This lack of higher-order skills was most apparent in test items measuring inferential comprehension in reading, problem solving in nonroutine situations in mathematics, persuasive writing involving logic and analysis, and scientific understandings in the physical sciences. With this established, the panels addressed the most difficult task of all: proposing steps to be taken to correct these problems.

What Can Be Done to Improve Higher-Order Learning?

Within the Classrooms. Any efforts to improve students' acquisition of more complex, higher-order cognitive skills must be based on appreciable restructuring of objectives and activities within the classroom. At a minimum, these suggestions from the NAEP panels should be considered:

1. Teachers should create more learning situations that require students to formulate, explain, and defend their opinions at some length. These should include both discussion activities among students and extensive, painstakingly evaluated writing activities.

2. Student ideas should be evaluated constructively. The method of presentation of those ideas — written or oral — should also be evaluated, but the emphasis should be on the ideas and logic students use.

3. It is important that regular assignments be given to students that require them to plan lines of inquiry for a relatively complex topic. If done effectively, students should also be able to lead a discussion of that topic for their classmates.

4. More frequent use should be made of "questioning/discovery" strategies in teaching, allowing the student to be less of a spectator and more of a participant. Such strategies have been used successfully for developing conceptual skills in mathematics and science.

5. Teachers can add freshness to their instruction by using an interdisciplinary approach to content. Undoubtedly the application of reading, writing, and mathematics to science and social studies will stimulate learning in all areas at all grade levels.

6. Students do best when teacher expectations are high. Even young children can learn large amounts of difficult material if it is expected of them. In mathematics, for example, problem-solving experiences should not be deferred until computational skills are mastered. Problem-

solving activity reinforces the learning of computational skills and provides meaning for their application. This will require a variety of teaching strategies, since those used to inculcate higher-order skills are not the same as those used for lower-order skills.

7. Teachers must make a concerted effort to reduce the class time that is consumed by routine administrative housekeeping tasks — tasks not directly related to student learning. This will increase the amount of academic learning time, which in turn will lead to improved achievement. In this way the central business of the classroom will be served better.

8. Students should have the opportunity to learn a variety of ways of analyzing reading material in order to find evidence for their opinions. They need instruction in alternative problem-solving approaches, and practice in formally applying these alternatives with different types of reading material.

9. Students need time in order to generate ideas for writing. They also need practice in organizing their ideas with respect to logic and structure. Writing need not be a solitary experience. Brainstorming in group discussions can spur a student's ideas and assist in the process of sorting and evaluating them. The written product can be shared with the group later.

10. Students should be required to write for meaningful purposes, with a specific audience in mind. In this way they will learn how to select and apply the most effective writing styles for a particular situation.

11. Students should be regularly challenged to apply mathematics to problem situations, ideally ones that are very realistic for them. They need to determine which mathematical operation must be used to solve each problem and to discover whether it is the most appropriate choice.

12. The textbooks and supplementary teaching materials selected should have a strong emphasis on higher-level cognitive objectives. Standard texts should be extended by the classroom teacher with learning activities that reflect the local environment and common student experiences.

13. Insofar as possible, the achievement testing program used should reflect the classroom emphasis on learning higher-order cognitive skills. Also, the evaluation of complex student work products (for ex-

ample, a critical essay or a science exhibit) should focus on the degree to which these skills are being learned. Evaluation of academic progress should be continuous and take place for all students immediately after they perform any learning exercise.

These are only some of the many suggestions that were made by panel members to improve achievement in higher-order cognitive skills. The suggestions are far more comprehensive than assessment data alone would justify, but they are well supported by both practice and the research regarding effective instruction. Adhering to these suggestions, it is argued, will have a positive influence on the quality of instruction in general and especially in the teaching of higher-level objectives.

Within the Schools and Communities. The effectiveness of any teacher is constrained by the environment of the school. There is a limit to how much can be accomplished in a given classroom, and that limit is determined by many factors — including the school climate — which can appreciably enhance or inhibit a teacher's effectiveness.

Studies of effective schools are numerous, and their conclusions help us to understand many of the actions that should be taken by the school and the community to improve student learning. Here are some of the major recommendations addressed to school systems and their communities that have been developed from research findings:

1. Every school should have a clearly articulated statement of mission that gives the teaching and administrative staffs a common understanding of instructional goals, priorities, assessment procedures, and accountability systems. For example, the mission statement might have a strong commitment to integrate critical thinking in each learning area. The staff would then undertake a series of steps based on this commitment to make it a part of today's operation and tomorrow's plans.

2. The principal of each school must be the instructional leader of that unit and must effectively communicate the mission of the school to the staff, students, and parents. To do so, the principal needs to understand and apply the tenets of instructional effectiveness in the management of the educational program.

3. It is absolutely necessary that parents understand and support the basic mission of the school and be given the opportunity to play an important role in helping the school achieve this mission. This means that a

vigorous effort must be made to strengthen the role of parents as teachers of their children in all learning areas including those that are highly school-specific, such as mathematics and science.

At a minimum we should develop more "learning contracts" involving students, teachers, and parents. If all share in the design and execution of the learning plan for the student, then all will share also in the success or failure that follows. The respective roles of all parties will be better defined and the assignment of accountability better established. Parents should have the opportunity to participate as full partners in the formal as well as the informal education of their children.

4. Each school needs an orderly, purposeful atmosphere that is free from the threat of physical harm, yet is not oppressive. It is essential that the climate be conducive to teaching and learning; little learning takes place amid disorder.

Beyond these recommendations to improve learning in classrooms and to enhance the school climate in general, there are other steps to be taken in the pursuit of better schools. Six of these steps are presented below.

1. Special educational programs to assist disadvantaged students are needed. NAEP data repeatedly reveal major improvements in achievement in the last decade by black and Hispanic students as well as by economically disadvantaged youth in general. No one knows all of the reasons for these gains, but the educational entitlement programs of the 1970s, such as the Title I program of the Elementary and Secondary Education Act and the "Right-to-Read" program, seem to have contributed substantially. With this circumstantial evidence in their favor, it is reasonable to support actively programs like these and to press for their continuation.

2. Instruction in basic skills should include higher-order learning. An emphasis on basic skills without attention to higher-order cognitive learning will probably yield higher achievement test scores initially, but this could prove to be counterproductive. A commitment to give students a better command of the basic skills certainly includes the more complex skills of communication and mathematics. We should teach the basic skills accordingly, emphasizing higher-level objectives in these areas.

3. High school enrollments in mainstream science, mathematics, English, government, and foreign language courses should be increased. Currently, enrollments in these courses are too low and are declining. Students are commonly permitted to ignore these learning areas or to seek soft replacements, some complete with unofficial frivolous titles ("Ecology for Poets," "French for Lovers").

At the same time that high school graduation requirements must be increased so that more learning areas are studied seriously, continuous efforts must also be made to maintain up-to-date curriculum materials and state-of-the-art equipment. This is particularly important for instruction in the sciences, because students entering these courses are faced with learning concepts involving high levels of abstraction; the courses are difficult for many, and discouragement, if not failure, is often the result.

4. More effective and better coordinated inservice education programs must be installed — programs that stress teacher achievement in content areas at least as much as teaching techniques. Concurrently, teachers must continually stay abreast of the latest delivery systems, especially those that are computer-based. Disconcerting evidence exists that many teachers are inadequately trained in the subjects they are teaching. Alarming examples of this exist in mathematics and science at all grade levels.

5. Career ladders should be established in the elementary and secondary schools. Crude as they are, such ladders work successfully in higher education. Why should they not be established for teachers at all grade levels and include differential salary levels based on merit?

A ladder of three, four, or more levels could be established with appropriate criteria and advancement procedures, along with sizable differences in remuneration at the various levels. It would be quite reasonable for master teachers to receive three times the salary of those teachers in the early years of their careers.

To move up the ladder, teachers would need career development opportunities tailored to their needs and the needs of the school. These opportunities would include not only conventional inservice activities but also short-term training programs; long-term exchanges with commerce, industry, government, and universities; and sabbatical leaves for intensive study. Steps such as these would go far to transform teaching into the true profession it should be.

6. A collegial spirit among students, teachers, principals, and parents must be established. This will help to reduce the adversarial relationships that now commonly exist. Perhaps we should establish a modified version of the Japanese quality circle in our schools.

Whatever the plan, participation in the governance of schools should be broadened. When teachers, administrators, students, parents, and other citizens have a voice in determining school policies and operations, they feel a sense of *ownership*. Such ownership gives all parties involved a stake in the performance of the school and leads to a feeling of success within each individual participating. A sense of ownership is a major ingredient in the recipe for a successful school.

Additional recommendations for the improvement of schools could be made, but the agenda for renewal is already heavy. Rather than add to it, let us begin now to orchestrate a winning combination of enthusiasm, dedication, energy, creativity, and resources needed to implement the necessary reforms.

The Road Ahead

It is easy to be pessimistic about today's schools. When selected parts of NAEP data (for example, achievement losses by 17-year-olds) are added to mountains of data from other sources including selected anecdotal evidence, one can find innumerable reasons for believing that our schools are doing a poor job and that there is little hope for improvement. But, as always, there is a flip side to such an analysis of NAEP data. Other parts of the assessment data (for example, achievement gains by disadvantaged youngsters), coupled with favorable anecdotal evidence, yield a more positive conclusion. We know of many effective programs going on in the schools, and these can provide a basis for mounting efforts to improve academic programs.

Renewal of our schools must start at the local level and move upward and outward from there. Practical plans for improvement must take shape within each individual school building. If this does not happen, very little change of importance will result in the total school system. For each school to serve as a mainspring for renewal, a number of conditions must be satisfied. To paraphrase John Gardner, each school must:

1. Create a hospitable environment for each participant and stakeholder
2. Establish built-in mechanisms for self-criticism
3. Develop a fluid internal structure
4. Develop a strong system of internal communication
5. Combat the process by which staff members become prisoners of their procedures and rules
6. Combat the vested interests that have grown up within it
7. Emphasize what it is going to become, rather than what it has been
8. Create an environment in which all concerned believe that it really makes a difference to the educational process whether they do well or badly, that everyone cares
9. Maintain an effective program to recruit staff members and develop their talents.

In short, each school must take many steps to strengthen itself internally, thereby creating an attitude among all participants that their actions count and will be recognized. Given the will to do so, they collectively can change the school significantly, and in the process achieve the goals they have set. To the degree that the school succeeds, society succeeds; to the degree that it fails, society fails.

In the beginning, renewal efforts will yield improvement at the margins. But continuous renewal efforts — the only kind worth talking about seriously — can produce startling changes. As educators plan to renew their schools continuously, they should consider the risk of "high failure" rather than be satisfied with "low success," which is nothing more than buying success cheaply by setting modest goals and reaching them in a short time without much effort. In contrast, setting challenging goals and allocating considerable effort and time to achieve them increases the risk of failure. Should "high failure" occur, it should not necessarily be viewed with dismay; it might actually represent a larger change for the better than "low success."

In the last analysis, we may have no choice but to establish ambitious renewal goals. Profound changes are now taking place in our society to which schools must respond. It is becoming increasingly clear, for example, that we are experiencing a "megashift" from an industrial-based society to an information-based one, in which there is a declining emphasis on the manufacture of goods and a concurrent emergence of an economy based on the gathering, organizing, and selling of information. More and more of our society is becoming "knowledge-intensive," and the "information business" is the fastest growing sector of the economy. In words of one NAEP report:

> Skills in reducing data, interpreting it, packaging it effectively, documenting decisions, explaining complex matters in simple terms and persuading are already highly prized in business, education and the military, and will become more so as the information explosion continues. They will also be increasingly important at personal and social levels. Quality of life is directly tied to our ability to think clearly amid the noise of modern life, to sift through all that competes for our attention until we find what we value, what will make our lives worth living. What we value is seldom on the surface and, when it is found, can seldom be defended from the incursions of the trivial without sustained efforts to understand it more deeply, to clarify its nature and to explain it to ourselves and others.
>
> (*Reading, Thinking and Writing*, 1981, p. 5)

Are most of our high school graduates prepared to enter the information society now unfolding? Definitely not. To prepare them properly will require sustained renewal efforts incorporating many of the suggestions and recommendations summarized above. As these efforts gain momentum, achievement scores will rise. But we should not luxuriate in feelings of self-satisfaction when this occurs. Test data are just indicators, not ends in themselves. The scope of school renewal is far more complex than that which is revealed by improved test scores.

The true payoff of successful renewal programs will be a steadily increasing number of high school graduates who can display evidence of higher-order achievement in a wide variety of learning areas. Indeed, perhaps we will be lucky enough to find a few graduates who resemble the fabled "Renaissance Man," seasoned with a dash of "world-class gymnast" and a pinch of "renowned stage actor." Impossible? Maybe, but we won't know how close we can come if we fail to try.

Annotated Bibliography

Ahmann, J. S. "Differential Changes in Levels of Achievement for Students in Three Age Groups." *Educational Studies* 10 (1979): 35-51.

NAEP data clearly show that pronounced differential changes in levels of achievement are occurring nationally. The most promising learning area is reading; the most promising age group is 9-year-olds. The least promising learning areas are, for the most part, mathematics and science; the least promising age group is 17-year-olds. Differential changes in achievement can be caused by school variables and societal variables; probably the former are the primary cause, especially for learning areas such as mathematics and science which are highly school-specific.

Goodlad, J. I. *A Place Called School.* New York: McGraw-Hill, 1983.

An ambitious research effort entitled "A Study of Schooling" provides a kind of holistic understanding of schools by studying the individual dynamics of a number of schools, including both environmental factors and school factors. Although school-to-school variations existed, a pervasive sameness was found in goal statements, instruction, the substance and design of curriculum, and the passivity of students during instruction. To change the status quo, the structure of the school needs to be changed. A step in this direction is to organize schools into largely self-sufficient four-year units of small size (100 students in an elementary unit and 160 in a secondary unit) with an appropriate professional staff to diagnose student learning difficulties and plan intervention and evaluation strategies. The staffing of each unit would include a head teacher, career teachers, aides, and interns; the success of school improvement would depend primarily on the work of this group.

Hodgkinson, H. L. "What's Still Right with Education." *Phi Delta Kappan* 64 (December 1982):231-35.

The 1970s was a period of "psychic recession" in which most citizens lost faith in many things including their schools. Now this feeling is beginning to reverse itself. Public support for schools is rising. Within the schools more emphasis is being placed on strong leadership from the principal, high expectations for all students, an orderly atmosphere, and frequent diagnostic evaluation of student progress. We should anticipate excellent performance in the elementary schools in the future, but the secondary schools will have to undergo some drastic changes if they are to serve their proper role in the preparation of workers to enter jobs in an information/service-based economy.

Husen, T. "Are Standards in U.S. Schools Really Lagging Behind Those in Other Countries?" *Phi Delta Kappan* 64 (March 1983):455-61.
The top 5% to 10% of the students finishing their secondary education in a comprehensive system like that in the United States perform academically at nearly the same level as their age-mates in selective systems in countries such as France, England, or Germany. In addition, those who are less able have a better opportunity to develop their potential in a comprehensive system. By itself, however, education cannot serve as an equalizer. The most serious problem faced by schools on both sides of the Atlantic is the rise of a new educational underclass composed of disadvantaged students who give up competing for success early in their school careers and suffer the consequences as adults in an information-based economy.

Maeroff, G. I. *Don't Blame the Kids: The Trouble with America's Public Schools.* New York: McGraw-Hill, 1982.
Rather than blame students for the problems in our educational system, we should reexamine our unrealistic expectation that schools must be "all things to all people." Whatever the social or personal problem, schools are supposed to solve it, yet they must raise levels of student achievement higher and higher. To make matters worse, the general public is critical of its schools, and parents are apathetic. Reform of the schools is possible, of course, and it will require a rededication to their basic academic mission coupled with close attention to the application in the classroom of research findings about effective instruction.

National Assessment of Educational Progress. *Reading, Thinking and Writing.* Denver, Colo.: Education Commission of the States, 1981.
By age 17, most students read a range of material appropriate for their age level, but about 10% are unable to read even simple materials. Moreover, the evidence cited by teenage students to support their assertions about what they read does not reflect effective strategies for approaching a text. The overwhelming majority lacked strategies for analyzing or evaluating material in order to deepen their understanding of what they read.